Are We Recycling?
A VIDEO INVESTIGATION

by Becky Cheston
illustrated by Michelle Gengaro

Harcourt
SCHOOL PUBLISHERS

Requests for permission to make copies of any part of the work should be addressed to School Permissions and Copyrights, Harcourt, Inc., 6277 Sea Harbor Drive, Orlando, Florida 32887–6777. Fax: 407-345-2418.

HARCOURT and the Harcourt Logo are trademarks of Harcourt, Inc., registered in the United States of America and/or other jurisdictions.

Printed in China

ISBN 10:   0-15-377432-0
ISBN 13:   978-0-15-377432-4

Ordering Options
ISBN 10:   0-15-377149-6 (Grade 5 Collection)
ISBN 13:   978-0-15-377149-1 (Grade 5 Collection)
ISBN 10:   0-15-377891-1 (package of 5)
ISBN 13:   978-0-15-377891-9 (package of 5)

2 3 4 5 6 7 8 9 10   0940   17 16 15 14 13 12 11 10 09

Setting: The Kennedy Elementary School cafeteria at lunchtime

Narrator: Julia, Matt, Fiona, and Will are students creating a video. Let's listen in on their project.

Julia: Hi. I'm Julia Morales from Mr. Green's science class. I am reporting to you live from Kennedy Elementary School. We're here today to investigate how well those at our school are complying with the recycling program—right, Will?

Will: That's right, Julia. I'm Will Bingham. During this video, Julia and I will visit selected areas of the school— unannounced—to see who's following the recycling rules and who's not.

Julia: The cafeteria is a good place to start because—

3

Narrator: Suddenly, another student, Charlie, enters.

Charlie: Hi, everyone! I thought we were meeting outside.

Matt: CUT!

Charlie: Oops! Sorry.

Fiona: What are you doing here?

Charlie: I was out sick all last week when everyone broke into groups. Mr. Green assigned me to your group. Is it too late for me to help out with the filming?

Fiona: We need someone to take notes and log the footage.

Narrator: Ms. Henson approaches the students.

Ms. Henson: Shouldn't you all be in class?

Fiona: Show her the permission slip, Matt!

Ms. Henson: Let me see. Mr. Green is letting his students bask in the halls during an entire double period?

Will: We're finishing up our video projects on altruism. Ours is on recycling here at school.

Ms. Henson: That sounds like a good topic. Well, just try not to get in anyone's way.

Fiona: She almost seemed compassionate after we told her the topic. She must care about recycling.

Charlie: Can someone give me a brief rundown of what we're doing here?

Will: Sure. We're supposed to make an educational video about things we can all do to avoid mistreating the earth. We chose recycling.

Julia: What's different about our group is that our video isn't just educational—it's also investigative.

Charlie: What are we investigating?

Julia: Whether or not the school will follow the district's recycling program.

Matt: Okay, can we begin again? Julia, the camera is on you. Ready—three, two, one, ACTION!

Julia: The cafeteria is a good place to start because right here, next to this conveyor belt, is where students dispose of their trash.

Will: Let's zoom in on these four big bins. They're color-coded and clearly labeled. This white one says PAPER for paper trash like lunch bags. If we look inside, we see paper and three cans! Those should go in this blue bin labeled CANS. A quick peek in this one shows us a bunch of cans, and—surprise! Plastic bottles!

Julia: Well, Will—those should go in this red bin, labeled PLASTIC. Over here, in this green bin, is where leftover food and other non-recyclables go.

Will: There you have it, folks. It seems like recycling in our school cafeteria has become sloppy. Perhaps we need a recycling mentor who can set an example and coordinate our recycling efforts.

Julia: Let's turn our attention now to another location. Let's take an excursion to the teachers' lounge.

Matt: CUT! That was great, people!

Narrator: The investigative team walks down the hall to the teachers' lounge. They peer through the doorway.

Charlie: Can you see if anyone's in there?

Julia: I detect Ms. Wong. She's getting a cup of coffee. There's Mr. Travis, our gym teacher.

Fiona: I could tell he was there without even looking. Oh, I loathe how he always jingles his keys in his pocket.

Matt: Come on—I'll do the talking.

Narrator: The students walk into the lounge and approach Ms. Wong and Mr. Travis.

Matt: Um, excuse me? We're making a video on recycling. Do you mind if we take some footage in here?

Mr. Travis: Well, I don't know. What exactly is your movie advocating?

Will: We're just investigating recycling in different parts of the school.

Mr. Travis: Well, I'm not sure that it is such a good idea to film in this room—in its present condition. It could use some tidying up, and these old couches are rather dilapidated.

Charlie: We're not really focusing on any of that.

Will: We just want to see how the school recycling program is going. In fact—Mr. Travis, would you mind being in the video for us?

Mr. Travis: Not at all. What do you want me to do?

Will: It's easy—just act animated, with a lot of fervor.

Matt: All right, then—is everyone ready? Let's go, people: three, two, one—ACTION!

Will: Our next segment comes to you from our own teachers' lounge. I have Mr. Travis here with me. Thanks for taking the time to help us out today, Mr. Travis.

Narrator: Will, Julia, and Mr. Travis begin to walk over to the recycling center in the teachers' lounge.

Matt: CUT! Um, Mr. Travis—do you think you could take your keys out of your pocket? That jingling noise . . . well, it's messing up the sound quality.

Mr. Travis: Oh! Sorry, I do that when I'm feeling giddy, and this is a lot of fun.

Narrator: Mr. Travis takes his keys out of his pocket and places them on a table.

Matt: Thanks. Now let's start again—ACTION!

Mr. Travis: We decided to put our recycling center by the coffee station since that's the most bustling place in the teachers' lounge. Mrs. Pittal thought of it, and we all agreed that it was an enterprising idea. As you can see, we have four barrels. Oh, my—are you sure you want to do that?

Will: Fiona's just zooming in on the contents so that we can get the inside scoop on how you're doing.

Mr. Travis: We just cleaned out the refrigerator. There are moldy leftovers in there. You're going to *scoop* that?

Will: Not literally. How does it look, Julia?

Julia: From what I can see, it looks like our teachers are doing a good job.

Mr. Travis: Thanks to Ms. Wong here. She is the most vital part of the teachers' recycling program.

Julia: Really? Would you care to comment on that for us, Ms. Wong?

Ms. Wong: Certainly. When people get careless about putting things in their proper place, I correct them.

Julia: That concludes our segment on recycling in the teachers' lounge.

Narrator: Now the students walk over to the auditorium to investigate.

Charlie: This auditorium is a great location for the video!

Fiona: I know. I love these sleek carved wood panels on the side of the stage. I should get a shot of that.

Matt: Fiona—it's cool that you have such a great artistic sensibility. However, that's not really the focus of our video.

Fiona: Just because we're talking about recycling doesn't mean our video has to look bland.

Julia: We're shooting backstage, anyway. There are lots of old sets and costumes you could include in the shot, Fiona.

Will: Wow, now that's a giant garbage barrel over there. Is that it, though?

Charlie: Where are all the recycle bins?

Julia: I don't know, but we should probably have this conversation on camera. Are you ready, Fiona?

Matt: Okay—everybody ready *now*? And—ACTION!

Julia: For our final segment, we take you backstage in the school auditorium.

Will: That's right, Julia. A lot of action takes place here. Students attend drama classes and choir practice. Also, stage crews for our many school productions build sets and make costumes in this area.

Julia: We're standing here in front of a lone trash barrel. Our policy says that every location must recycle items in the separate bins that the school provides.

Will: However, those bins are nowhere to be found. Fiona, why don't you zoom in on this solitary barrel—I'm willing to bet that recycling is not taking place here.

Julia: You're right, Will. I'm looking at lots of crumpled papers, a couple of juice cans, an empty plastic water bottle, half a sandwich, a banana peel—

Will: I think we've seen enough. Fiona, can you pan the camera around the backstage area? Maybe we can find out where the recycle bins went.

Julia: As everyone can see, they've simply disappeared.

Will: Wait a minute! Fiona—hold the camera right there, on those set pieces. See those stools—and that clock? Do they look familiar?

Julia: Wow—you're right! They're made out of broken recycle bins! The damaged bins were never replaced.

Will: There's no recycling here—just plenty of props.

Julia: Good job spotting the mistreatment of our school's recycle bins, Will!

Will: Thank you, Julia. Well, folks, that's our final segment. I think we can conclude from these sample locations that our school needs to dedicate itself to the recycling program.

Matt: CUT!

Will and Julia: What now?

Matt: Nothing. It's a wrap!

Think Critically

1. What is the focus of this group's video project?

2. From Matt's lines in the story, what conclusion can you draw about his role in the video project? Explain.

3. Did you enjoy this story? Why or why not?

4. Summarize what happens in this story.

5. What is the author's purpose for writing this story?

 **Language Arts**

Investigation Continues Imagine that these students are investigating another area of the school. Write a new scene in the same style as this Readers' Theater.

School-Home Connection Explain the situation presented in this play to a family member. Discuss the recycling practices in your area. List ways to improve your own recycling habits.

Word Count: 1,486